Table of Contents

T0052531

Pebble®

Families

Grandmothers

Revised and Updated

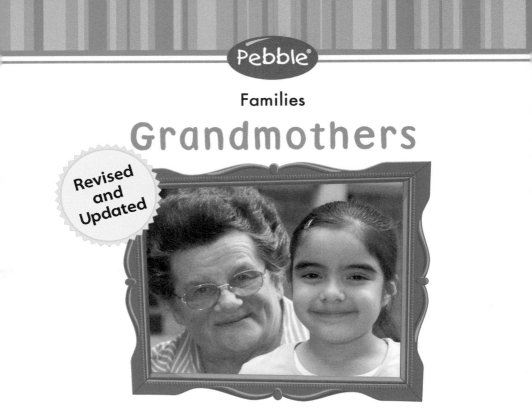

by Lola M. Schaefer

Consulting Editor: Gail Saunders-Smith, PhD

Capstone press®
Mankato, Minnesota

Pebble Books are published by Capstone Press,
1710 Roe Crest Drive, North Mankato, Minnesota 56003.
www.capstonepub.com

Library of Congress Cataloging-in-Publication Data
Schaefer, Lola M., 1950–
   Grandmothers/by Lola M. Schaefer. — Rev. and updated.
   p. cm. — (Pebble books. Families)
   Includes bibliographical references and index.
   Summary: "Simple text and photographs present grandmothers and how they
interact with their families" — Provided by publisher.
   ISBN-13: 978-1-4296-1226-5 (hardcover)
   ISBN-10: 1-4296-1226-6 (hardcover)
   ISBN-13: 978-1-4296-1755-0 (softcover)
   ISBN-10: 1-4296-1755-1 (softcover)
   1. Grandmothers — Juvenile literature. 2. Grandmothers — Pictorial works—
Juvenile literature. I. Title. II. Series.
HQ759.9.S35 2008
306.874'5 — dc22   2007027097

Note to Parents and Teachers

The Families set supports national social studies standards related
to identifying family members and their roles in the family. This
book describes and illustrates grandmothers. The images support
early readers in understanding the text. The repetition of words
and phrases helps early readers learn new words. This book also
introduces early readers to subject-specific vocabulary words, which
are defined in the glossary section. Early readers may need some
assistance to read some words and to use the Table of Contents,
Glossary, Read More, Internet Sites, and Index sections of the book.

Grandmothers

Grandmothers are mothers of fathers and mothers.

Grandmothers
have grandchildren.

8

Busy Grandmothers

Grandmothers are busy.
Grandma Jane works
at a library.

Grandma Lynn paints.

Grandma Nancy
bakes cakes.

At Play

Grandmothers have fun.

Grandma Vera plays tennis.

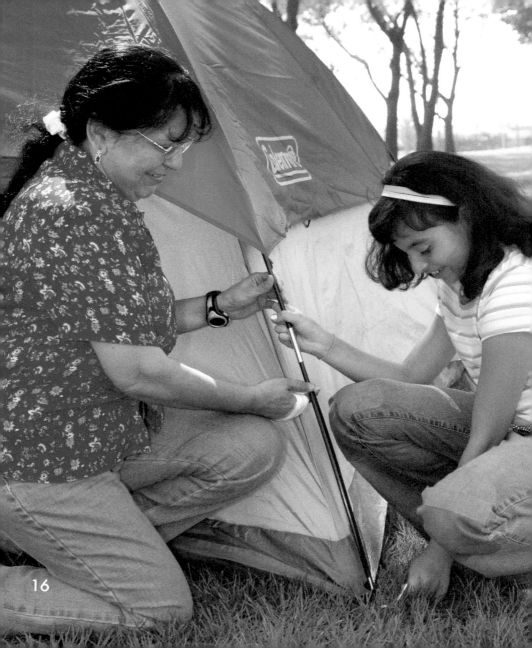

Grandma Amelia takes
Paulina camping.

Grandma Martha teaches Jenny to ride a bike.

Grandmothers love
their grandchildren.

Glossary

father — a male parent; your dad's mother is your grandmother.

grandchildren — the children of a grandmother's son or daughter.

mother — a female parent; your mom's mother is your grandmother.

teach — to show someone how to do something new; grandparents often teach their grandchildren new things as they grow up.

Lord, Janet. *Here Comes Grandma!* New York: Henry Holt, 2005.

Parr, Todd. *The Grandma Book.* New York: Little, Brown, 2006.

Internet Sites

FactHound offers a safe, fun way to find Internet sites related to this book. All of the sites on FactHound have been researched by our staff.

Here's how:

1. Visit *www.facthound.com*
2. Choose your grade level.
3. Type in this book ID **1429612266** for age-appropriate sites. You may also browse subjects by clicking on letters, or by clicking on pictures and words.
4. Click on the **Fetch It** button.

FactHound will fetch the best sites for you!

Index

Word Count: 50
Grade 1
Early-Intervention Level: 10

Editorial Credits
Sarah L. Schuette, revised edition editor; Kim Brown, revised edition designer

Photo Credits
Capstone Press, cover; Karon Dubke, interiors